Daily Prayer
Seeking the Heart of God

Berenice Aguilera

For my family

Check out
www.bereniceaguilera.com
for your free copy of
Daily Prayer through the Ten Commandments.

Contents

Introduction

Prayer can be hard, can't it?

What do we say?

We thank God for the day ahead, ask him to bless our family, help us in our work and... we fizzle out. We want to say more but don't really know what.

We know God hears even our weakest prayers, but we want more...

The intent of this prayer-book is to help with just that.

These prayers are not intended to be used in a ritualistic way. These are not magical words to get God to listen to you (He always listens to you); rather they are intended as an encouragement to your own prayer life.

As you pray the prayers on the following pages, the Holy Spirit will work in your heart and give you your own words to say, or ideas of things you need to pray for.

When that happens, just let the words flow, and speak those things that come to mind.

May God grant you grace and perseverance, as you seek His face.

A Blameless Walk

PSALM 119:1-8

Blessed are those whose way is blameless, who walk in the law of the Lord!

Blessed are those who keep his testimonies, who seek him with their whole heart, who also do no wrong, but walk in his ways!

You have commanded your precepts to be kept diligently. Oh that my ways may be steadfast in keeping your statutes! Then I shall not be put to shame, having my eyes fixed on all your commandments.

I will praise you with an upright heart when I learn your righteous rules. I will keep your statutes; do not utterly forsake me!

Father, the desire of my heart is to love you and to know you more. I want to walk according to your law, and I seek you with all my heart. Lord God I find it so hard sometimes to just sit down and read your Word. I feel as if I am stagnating, and I don't want that. I just don't feel that I'm growing in you.

I want the things I read in your Word to be true in my life. As I read about men and women of faith Father, that is how I want my life to be. I want to walk according to your word. I want to be rich in the knowledge of you.

I know that this desire for you can only come from you. I can't manufacture it with my own strength. So Father in the name of Jesus, I ask you to fill my heart with your Spirit. Fill my heart with the knowledge of you. Lord I want more of you.

I pray in this time ahead, that I will grow in knowing you. I pray that my desire will be for you. I pray that as I go through today that I will bless those that I meet and that I will bring a sense of your presence into their lives.

Help me to have an obedient heart in everything, whether it be in my speech or in my action or in my thoughts. And I pray Lord that you'll make me aware when I'm grieving you. Sometimes I just go forward without even thinking or even realizing I am doing wrong. Forgive me for the times when I have done this.

I pray in Jesus name that you will guide me today, that you will fill me with your Spirit and that I will know you more in Jesus name I pray, Amen.

Teach me Your Ways

PSALM 119:33-36

Teach me, O LORD, the way of your
statutes; and I will keep it to the end.
Give me understanding, that I may keep
your law and observe it with my whole
heart. Lead me in the path of your
commandments, for I delight in it.
Incline my heart to your testimonies,
and not to selfish gain!

I love you Lord. Thank you for this new day. Thank you for revealing yourself to me so that I might come to know you. Thank you that you have saved me.

I pray that you will work in my heart that I may love your ways. I pray that my heart will only desire to do your will and that nothing I do might be done for selfish gain.

I pray that you will forgive me the times I have

spoken without thought, for the times when I have ignored you and gone my own way. This is not what I want, and not how I wish to live. I desire above all things that my eyes would be firmly fixed on you. I pray that you will continue to turn my heart towards you. I pray that you will cause my heart to crave your presence. I want more of you in my life.

Direct me in your paths for I know that the times I have been obedient to you have been the times where I have found most delight in you. O God, turn my eyes away from worthless things, preserve my life according to your word.

Change my heart O Lord. If I am blind, give me sight. If I am deaf, give me hearing. I want to see and hear you.

I pray that I will love your word more and more each day. Please give me understanding in both my mind and in my heart. Draw me to you. Increase my faith, that I might believe.

I commit this day into your hands. Do with me as you will. Let my speech be seasoned with your grace, and let my heart be full of your love for those around me. I pray this in Jesus Name, Amen.

Earnestly I Seek You

PSALM 63:1-8

You, God, are my God, earnestly I seek you; I thirst for you, my whole being longs for you, in a dry and parched land where there is no water. I have seen you in the sanctuary and beheld your power and your glory. Because your love is better than life, my lips will glorify you. I will praise you as long as I live, and in your name I will lift up my hands. I will be fully satisfied as with the richest of foods; with singing lips my mouth will praise you. On my bed I remember you; I think of you through the watches of the night. Because you are my help, I sing in the shadow of your wings. I cling to you; your right hand upholds me.

Thank you Lord for this new day. Thank you that I am never alone, that you are always with me. O God, you are my Lord and my God, and I will seek you with all my heart. My soul thirsts for you. I need you Father as a starving man needs food, as a man dying of thirst needs water.

Father, I have caught glimpses of you, glimpses of your power, glimpses of your glory, but it is not enough. I want to know you more. I want to see more of your power at work in my life. I want to see more of your glory at work in my life.

Thank you for your presence, for your love is greater than anything I've ever known.

Father, I want to learn how to seek you with all of my heart and with all of my soul. God, I want to see you. I want to see your strength at work in my life. I want to seek your face always.

You say in your word that anyone who asks, receives, and he who seeks will find, and to him who knocks the door will be opened. I am asking you to show me more of you. I am asking you to give me more understanding of your word. I am asking you to guide me into more truth.

Lord, I ask that you reveal more of yourself to me. I pray that you will fill me with your Holy Spirit. I pray that I will see more of you. Today I want to trust in you. Whatever decisions I need to make, whatever challenges I face, I want to trust you and I want to remember to bring them before you.

I want to walk in your wisdom. I pray that I will never deny you. I pray that should I be given an opportunity to tell others about you that I will not fear. I pray for courage and boldness to talk about you and your kingdom coming into my life. I pray that you will give me courage and boldness to speak about what you have done for me. I pray that you will give me the right words to say to those around me and that the words I read in the Bible will come to mind and I'll be able to speak out and explain them to other people.

I ask Lord as you reveal yourself to me, that you will use me in your service. I pray Lord for purity of heart. I pray today I will walk in your paths and that I will honor you in everything I say and in everything I do, in Jesus name, Amen.

Loving God

*Love the Lord your God with all your heart and
with all your soul and with all your strength.*

Lord, once I was dead in sin, but you came and had
mercy on me. You opened my heart, and I
understood your love for me. I understood that you
made a way for me to come to you, that you took my
sin, nailed it to the cross in Jesus and wiped away my
guilt forever.

Yet for all of this, I understand what you have done
in such a shallow way. I think of your mercy, yet my
heart is barely moved. I understand that my sins have
been removed from me yet I am not truly bothered.
I hate this shallowness of mine. I want a deeper
understanding of what you have done for me. I read
your word, but I want it to impact me through and
through, not just be as water off a ducks back.

I want to love you with all my heart, and with all of

my soul and with all of my strength. That is what I truly want. I know that any understanding that I have is because you have given it to me. I know that my heart, soul, and strength are in your hands. O God I want more. Help me to care more. Cause my heart to be desperate for you. Give me a hunger for your word and passion for your presence.

I don't truly understand what I have been saved from, as I know that if I did, I would be desperate to tell others about you. I know that if I truly understood the cost of my salvation, I would love the lost. And I don't. I want to, but I am not moved by their destiny of hell. O God, soften my heart, give me a heart that loves the lost, give me understanding of what you have done for me. In Jesus Name, Amen.

God of the Heavens

DEUTERONOMY 10:12-22

To the LORD your God belong the heavens, even the highest heavens, the earth and everything in it.

Yet the LORD set his affection on your ancestors and loved them, and he chose you, their descendants, above all the nations—as it is today. Circumcise your hearts, therefore, and do not be stiff-necked any longer.

For the LORD your God is God of gods and Lord of lords, the great God, mighty and awesome, who shows no partiality and accepts no bribes.

He defends the cause of the fatherless and the widow, and loves the foreigner residing among you, giving them food and clothing. And you are to love those who are foreigners, for you yourselves were foreigners in Egypt.

Fear the LORD your God and serve him. Hold fast to him and take your oaths in his name. He is the one you praise; he is your God, who performed for you those great and awesome

wonders you saw with your own eyes. Your
ancestors who went down into Egypt were
seventy in all, and now the LORD your God has
made you as numerous as the stars in the sky.

Father, by your Word you created the heavens and the earth. By your Word you sustain the universe. And by your Word you give me life. Thank you for your great and wonderful gift to me.

I pray that my life will bring you the glory you deserve. I pray that I will be a blessing to those around me, and that the richness of your mercy will be manifest towards them.

O God, I hunger after you, I thirst after you. My desire above everything is to serve you with all my heart and soul and to walk in your ways, even as did the saints of old.

I pray that you will reveal to me anything in my life that is hindering my drawing closer to you. I don't want it in my life. If there is anything I am hanging on to, anything I am blind to, please show me that I might repent and turn away. I want nothing in my life that will cause you dishonor.

Lord you defend the cause of the fatherless and the widow. When you walked this earth, you healed every person that came to you. You spoke wisdom where there was foolishness and unmasked the hypocrite. You showed love to everyone wherever you went. In you is all truth, and I want my life to reflect your truth. I want my life to be a reflection of your love for mankind.

As I read your Word, fill me with your Holy Spirit. Cause my understanding to be enlightened that I might know you more. Turn my heart from my own desires and guide me in your ways. In Jesus name I pray, Amen.

My Soul Yearns for You

How lovely is your dwelling place, Lord Almighty! My soul yearns, even faints, for the courts of the Lord; my heart and my flesh cry out for the living God.

Even the sparrow has found a home, and the swallow a nest for herself, where she may have her young— a place near your altar, LORD Almighty, my King and my God.

Blessed are those who dwell in your house; they are ever praising you.

Blessed are those whose strength is in you, whose hearts are set on pilgrimage. As they pass through the Valley of Baka, they make it a place of springs; the autumn rains also cover it with pools.

They go from strength to strength, till each appears before God in Zion.

Hear my prayer, LORD God Almighty; listen to me, God of Jacob. Look on our shield, O God;

*look with favor on your anointed one. Better is
one day in your courts than a thousand
elsewhere; I would rather be a doorkeeper in
the house of my God than dwell in the tents of
the wicked.*

*For the LORD God is a sun and shield; the LORD
bestows favor and honor; no good thing does he
withhold from those whose walk is blameless.
LORD Almighty, blessed is the one who trusts in
you.*

Lord God, you are my home. You are where I always want to be. This Psalm talks about the Psalmist yearning, even fainting for your courts, his heart and flesh crying out to you. God this is how I want my relationship with you to be. I want this yearning and longing for you. I can't make myself feel like this. I don't want an emotion, I want this to be real in me, not some kind of manufactured feeling.

O God, as I go about my work today, I pray that I will find strength in you. I pray that you will give me strength to control my tongue and be wise in my speech.

I pray that you will give me strength in my thought life, so that I might dwell only on good things. I pray that you will give me strength to believe that you are able to help me when all seems to go against me. Help me Lord in my times of unbelief. Help me to grow in faith. Help me to trust in you.

I know that it is true that 'better is one day in your courts than a thousand elsewhere.' Well, I pray that the influence of the world around me will grow less and less, and that my contentment will come from my relationship with you.

Lord you are light in my life, you guide my way. You protect me from the enemy and his plans to destroy. Thank you for all the good things in my life, I *will* trust in you in Jesus Name, Amen.

Consider the Lilies

MATTHEW 6:25-33

"Therefore, I tell you, do not be anxious about your life, what you will eat or what you will drink, nor about your body, what you will put on. Is not life more than food, and the body more than clothing?

Look at the birds of the air: they neither sow nor reap nor gather into barns, and yet your heavenly Father feeds them. Are you not of more value than they?

And which of you by being anxious can add a single hour to his span of life? And why are you anxious about clothing?

Consider the lilies of the field, how they grow: they neither toil nor spin, yet I tell you, even Solomon in all his glory was not arrayed like one of these.

But if God so clothes the grass of the field, which today is alive and tomorrow is thrown into the oven, will he not much more clothe you,

O you of little faith?

Therefore, do not be anxious, saying, 'What shall we eat?' or 'What shall we drink?' or 'What shall we wear?' For the Gentiles seek after all these things, and your heavenly Father knows that you need them all.

But seek first the kingdom of God and his righteousness, and all these things will be added to you.

"Therefore, do not be anxious about tomorrow, for tomorrow will be anxious for itself. Sufficient for the day is its own trouble."

Lord God, I commit this day into your hands. I commit my needs into your hands. You have promised to provide for me. You have promised to feed and clothe me, and I ask that you grant me faith to trust you. I know that by worrying over anything is not trusting you. But so often I find myself worrying and completely forgetting to bring my thoughts to you and trust you. I pray that should I worry about anything today, that you will bring to my mind my need to give this into your hands. I know that you are trustworthy, and I know that you above all are able to help me in all my needs.

O God teach me how to seek your kingdom first. Teach me about your righteousness. Change my heart to live for you and not for the things of this world. Change my heart so that I care about the way that I live enough to make changes. Lord, I want to truly trust you, I want to be able to let go of things that hold me back.

I pray Lord that my testimony will be one of living by faith in you. I want to be able to tell others how you have provided for me. I want to tell others instances of how you have worked in my life. I read about these in the Bible, and I read them in testimony books, and I know that sharing these things with those around can build up people's faith.

I pray that as I walk with you today, that you will make me aware of times and instances that I need to trust you, and where I need to be asking for your help.

Lord, I commit my worries into your hands. I commit my worries about tomorrow and the future into your hands. All I have is today. And I want this day to be one where I trust in you. I pray Lord that you will continue to open up my heart and continue to make me more aware of you. I pray that my faith in you will grow and that my testimony will bring honor to you in Jesus name, Amen.

Count it all Joy

"Therefore, everyone who hears these words of mine and puts them into practice is like a wise man who built his house on the rock. The rain came down, the streams rose, and the winds blew and beat against that house; yet it did not fall because it had its foundation on the rock.

But everyone who hears these words of mine and does not put them into practice is like a foolish man who built his house on sand. The rain came down, the streams rose, and the winds blew and beat against that house, and it fell with a great crash."

JAMES 1:2-6

Count it all joy, my brothers, when you meet trials of various kinds, for you know that the testing of your faith produces steadfastness. And let steadfastness have its full effect, that you may be perfect and complete, lacking in nothing.

19

If any of you lacks wisdom, let him ask God,
who gives generously to all without reproach,
and it will be given him. But let him ask in faith,
with no doubting, for the one who doubts is like
a wave of the sea that is driven and tossed by
the wind.

Father. I pray that my life will be one of putting your words into practice. I want to build my life on a firm foundation, and I know that it comes from your word. I want to be like the wise man who built his house on the rock.

I know that if I build my life on you, trouble can come, and you will always be with me. *You* are my foundation. I know that I am not alone.

Father, I pray that you will make me aware of times when I behave in a foolish manner. Make me aware when I am not believing and trusting you. I want no part of this in my life.

Teach me how to build my life on you. I know Lord that you will allow trials in our lives to strengthen our faith. I know my faith needs to be tested in order to develop perseverance. Your word speaks about perseverance finishing its work so that we may be made mature and complete not lacking anything.

I pray for perseverance in my life. I pray that I will not keep giving up every time there is a little difficulty. I pray God for this maturity to grow in my life so that I won't fall away because of difficulties or hardships. Lord I want to be walking with you to the last breath in my body.

Lord you give generously to all that ask of you and I pray Lord for wisdom to be present in my life. I ask you for a believing heart. Forgive me for the times I have not believed or trusted you.

I don't want to be like the man who doubts and is blown and tossed by the winds. Lord that person has no foundation and I really, really want my foundation to be strong and deep so that when I do go through times of trial I won't be swayed. I ask this in Jesus Name, Amen.

Unless the Lord...

PSALM 127:1

Unless the LORD builds the house, those who build it labor in vain.

Unless the LORD watches over the city, the watchman stays awake in vain.

MATTHEW 8:5-10

When he had entered Capernaum, a centurion came forward to him, appealing to him, "Lord, my servant is lying paralyzed at home, suffering terribly."

And he said to him, "I will come and heal him."

But the centurion replied, "Lord, I am not worthy to have you come under my roof, but only say the word, and my servant will be healed.

For I too am a man under authority, with soldiers under me. And I say to one, 'Go,' and he goes, and to another, 'Come,' and he comes, and to my servant, 'Do this,' and he does it."

When Jesus heard this, he marveled and said to those who followed him, "Truly, I tell you, with no one in Israel have I found such faith.

Unless the Lord builds the house, its builders labor in vain. I know this truth Lord and as I read the Bible, I want you to build your Word, your strength and your love in my life. Fill me with faith to believe your word.

I pray you will increase in me a desire for you. I love you so much Lord and yet I know that I understand so little.

I pray for times of quiet where I may just think on you. That I might meditate on your precepts, that I might learn more of you. I don't want knowledge *about* you, I want to know *you*.

As I look at this incident with the Centurion asking for his servant's healing, I see how he believed in you. I know that you are the giver of faith, and I know that his ability to believe came first from you. I pray that you will give me this faith.

I pray that you will guide me and show me when I need to step out and act in faith. My life seems to be filled with just the ordinary and mundane. Make me aware when I need to trust in you and not in my own strength.

I see in the Centurion such humility and a willingness to take direction and am aware that I give in so often to pride. So often I want my own way and rebel against going out of my way for others.

I pray that you will build commitment to your church into my life. I pray that my life will be full of service to my brothers and sisters in your family. I pray that you will give me gifts to use in your service, in Jesus Name I pray, Amen.

Whom Shall I Fear?

The LORD is my light and my salvation; whom shall I fear? The LORD is the stronghold of my life; of whom shall I be afraid?

MARK 4:21-23

And he said to them, "Is a lamp brought in to be put under a basket, or under a bed, and not on a stand? For nothing is hidden except to be made manifest; nor is anything secret except to come to light. If anyone has ears to hear, let him hear."

Lord, you are my light and my salvation, whom shall I fear? You are the stronghold of my life, of whom shall I be afraid? I thank you for today. Thank you for giving me breath in my body, thank you for all the good things you have given me in my life. Thank you for providing me with food to eat and clothes to cover my body. You have called me to be as a light on a lampstand. Your goodness and your mercy and loving-kindness were meant to be proclaimed to the world, not kept shut up and hidden.

Forgive me for those times I have failed to take the opportunity to share about you. Forgive me for the times when I have turned away whether it be from shyness or embarrassment, or lack of time or care.

You came and you saved me, and your desire is to save others around me. Give me grace and wisdom to take those opportunities. Give me the words to say. Teach me your salvation so that I might communicate it to others. Draw me close to you Father. I want to tell others about what you have done for me, but so often feel confused and mixed up when I am about to speak. Give me clarity of mind, give me crystal clear understanding of what it is that you have done for mankind.

Give me the ability to speak convincingly and fill me with your Holy Spirit so that what I speak will impact the lives of those around me. I pray that I will walk in your paths today and that I will be obedient to your will. I pray that your truth and love will shine through me to touch other people's lives. May your kingdom come into the lives of those around me. May you be glorified and your name lifted up in my life in Jesus Name, Amen.

God Works in You

PHILIPPIANS 2:12-16

*Therefore, my beloved, as you have always
obeyed, so now, not only as in my presence but
much more in my absence, work out your own
salvation with fear and trembling, for it is God
who works in you, both to will and to work for
his good pleasure.*

*Do all things without grumbling or disputing,
that you may be blameless and innocent,
children of God without blemish in the midst of
a crooked and twisted generation, among whom
you shine as lights in the world, holding fast to
the word of life, so that in the day of Christ I
may be proud that I did not run in vain or labor
in vain.*

Lord God, I commit this day into your hands. I pray
that you will be honored and glorified in my life.
You created all things and by your power all things
are held together. When I look up I see such beauty,

and when I look down I see such intricacy of design and order that my heart fills with worship. You created me to love and serve you.

I pray that my life might be characterized by obedience. So often I end up allowing my mouth to speak before I think of what I am saying. Help me Father to have control over my tongue. Help me to think before I speak. Make me aware of when I need to keep silent and then help me to *be* silent.

I want to be more like you. Full of wisdom and loving-kindness to those around me. I want people to see a testimony to you in my life. I long to hear the words 'Well done, good and faithful servant.'

It is you who gives me the will and ability to act according to your purposes. I pray that you will make me sensitive to your Holy Spirit. Help me to be aware of when you are trying to tell me something.

Forgive me for the times when I have complained about doing something. Help me to seize those moments and turn them round and learn self-control. Help me to be disciplined in my life.

I pray that my life will be one that holds out the Word of Life to those around me. Use me Father that I might tell others about you. Bring people across my path and give me the words to say to them to tell them about you. I pray all this in Jesus Name, Amen.

Let me not Deny You

MARK 14:66-72

And as Peter was below in the courtyard, one of the servant girls of the high priest came, and seeing Peter warming himself, she looked at him and said, "You also were with the Nazarene, Jesus."

But he denied it, saying, "I neither know nor understand what you mean." And he went out into the gateway and the rooster crowed.

And the servant girl saw him and began again to say to the bystanders, "This man is one of them." But again, he denied it.

And after a little while the bystanders again said to Peter, "Certainly you are one of them, for you are a Galilean."

But he began to invoke a curse on himself and to swear, "I do not know this man of whom you speak."

And immediately the rooster crowed a second time. And Peter remembered how Jesus had said to him, "Before the rooster crows twice, you will deny me three times." And he broke down and wept.

Lord, your works are faithful and just and your word is trustworthy. I pray that you will continue to open my eyes to your faithfulness. O God make me *aware* of your faithfulness.

I feel sometimes that I go around with blinkers on my eyes, only being able to see a narrow view. Open my understanding to your Word. I know that I can trust you, but I want to live it as well, not just know it in my mind.

I pray that even as you are faithful to me, I might be faithful to you. I pray that you will forgive me the times I have feared to acknowledge you before others.

I pray that you will forgive me for the times when I did not speak up and felt shame in sharing about you. This is not what I want in my life. Cleanse my heart.

I ask you that you give me courage to speak out and that I will never find myself in a position where I am denying you.

I pray that you will bring me into situations where I need to speak out about my faith in you. I pray that you will build faithfulness in me that I might be strong and steadfast in you. I pray for patience when I find things difficult. I pray that I will *remember* that you are with me and not live through hard times oblivious of your presence. Please help me Lord in Jesus Name, Amen.

Giver of Eternal Life

LUKE 18:18-22

And a ruler asked him, "Good Teacher, what must I do to inherit eternal life?"

And Jesus said to him, "Why do you call me good? No one is good except God alone. You know the commandments: 'Do not commit adultery, Do not murder, Do not steal, Do not bear false witness, honor your father and mother.'"

And he said, "All these I have kept from my youth."

When Jesus heard this, he said to him, "One thing you still lack. Sell all that you have and distribute to the poor, and you will have treasure in heaven; and come, follow me."

I thank you Father that you have given me eternal life. Thank you, Lord, that because of you I can now look forward to spending an eternity in your presence. I love you Lord.

Lord I want more of you. I pray again that you will give me more desire for your presence, more desire for your word and a heart to obey your will.

I pray that there will be nothing in my life that hinders my walk with you. I pray that you will reveal to me if there is anything that I am doing that keeps me from following you whole-heartedly. Give me a heart willing to do anything for you Lord. Change my character to be more like you.

How often I want my own way Lord. I see so much selfishness in my life and this is not what I want. I pray that you will forgive me for going my own way instead of looking to you. Please give me an awareness of when I am doing this so that I might turn away.

There are so many times when I have harboured in my heart resentment towards others. Times when I have not forgiven readily, and I ask your forgiveness for this. You have forgiven me and I know that I have no right to withhold forgiveness from others.

I ask forgiveness for the times when I have not believed you. For the times when I did not trust but instead, I doubted your word. I don't want this in my life. I want to trust you implicitly and act on that trust. I want my life to be one of complete surrender to you.

And I ask your forgiveness for the times I have

caused discord in my family or with my friends. I ask forgiveness as I did not care enough for them to put them first. I want my life to be one where I care deeply for those around me so that I might be careful not to hurt them with words or action.

I pray that nothing will hinder my walk with you in Jesus Name, Amen.

Hallowed be Your Name

MATTHEW 6:9

Our Father in heaven, hallowed be
your name.

Father, I thank you that you have made me your child. That you took me out of my godless life and revealed yourself to me, so that I might dwell with you forever.

I thank you that I can draw near to you in the confidence that I will be accepted, not for anything that I have done, but because of what you have done. Because of the sacrifice of your son for everything I ever did, and everything I ever will do against your will.

Lord I know that I don't deserve heaven. I know that I don't deserve your favor, but I thank you for it, and I accept it. I thank you for the gift of Jesus, that he took all the punishment that I deserve and removed my guilt before you forever.

I know that without you I would not be able to honor you. Every desire, and every inclination in me to turn toward you and trust you, comes from you. I pray that you will give me your grace that I might lift you up as I ought. I pray that you will reveal your sovereign power and majesty to me that I might all the more worship and adore you.

Make yourself known to me. I don't want ignorance of you to be a part of my life. Enlighten my mind to your glory, instruct me in your ways. Let every inclination in me be to think, speak and act according to what you have laid down in your Word in Jesus Name, Amen.

Your Kingdom Come

MATTHEW 6:10

*Your kingdom come, your will be done, on earth
as it is in heaven.*

I love you Lord, and I worship you. You alone are
worthy of all glory and honor. You alone deserve
praise.

Lord, I pray that your kingdom will continue to grow
in my life and in the lives of those around me. I thank
you that you have taken me out of Satan's power and
his kingdom of sin.

I pray that his plans for my life will come to nothing.
I pray that you will protect me from his influence in
my life.

I ask that I will be rich in the knowledge of your
gospel and that you will give me the grace to be able
to share it with others. Grant me daily more understanding of what you have done for me.

I know that the more I understand, the more influence it will have on my actions.

I pray that you will use me to encourage my brothers and sisters in the church. That by confirming your work on the cross I might be effective in giving comfort, and useful in building up those that love you.

I pray that you will rule in my heart. Rule my desires. Rule my thoughts and dreams, in Jesus Name, Amen.

Your Words are Tender
and True

JOHN 8:37-50

They answered him, "Abraham is our father."
Jesus said to them, "If you were Abraham's
children, you would be doing the works
Abraham did, but now you seek to kill me, a
man who has told you the truth that I heard
from God.

This is not what Abraham did. You are doing the
works your father did."

They said to him, "We were not born of sexual
immorality. We have one Father—even God."

Jesus said to them, "If God were your Father,
you would love me, for I came from God and I
am here. I came not of my own accord, but he
sent me. Why do you not understand what I say?

It is because you cannot bear to hear my word.
You are of your father the devil, and your will is
to do your father's desires. He was a murderer
from the beginning, and does not stand in the

truth, because there is no truth in him.

When he lies, he speaks out of his own character, for he is a liar and the father of lies. But because I tell the truth, you do not believe me.

Which one of you convicts me of sin? If I tell the truth, why do you not believe me? Whoever is of God hears the words of God. The reason why you do not hear them is that you are not of God."

The Jews answered him, "Are we not right in saying that you are a Samaritan and have a demon?" Jesus answered, "I do not have a demon, but I honor my Father, and you dishonor me. Yet I do not seek my own glory; there is One who seeks it, and he is the judge.

Father, your mercy is so tender and true. I am constantly amazed at your works. Once I belonged to the father of lies. He was my father and I followed in his footsteps. I was obedient to him and completely blind to my need of you. I loved doing his will, going my own way, doing my own thing in complete ignorance of you.

Yet you O God, looked upon me and loved me. You saw my need and my shame, and you revealed your Son to me. I saw how you had chosen to put the punishment I so deserved upon your Son so that I might be set free from sin and death. Words cannot express my gratitude to you my Lord. I love you with all my heart. I desire to serve you all the days of my life. Yet I know that my very desire comes from you. I honor you and glorify your name.

I ask you that you will give me wisdom to discern right from wrong. I ask for wisdom that I might discern your will and act on it.

I pray that you will rid my life of any blindness I might have towards you and forgive me for the times I have gone my own way and behaved in a manner that brings dishonor to you.

Lord be lifted up in my life. I ask for more love and more desire for you. Fill my heart with your Word and give me understanding in Jesus Name, Amen.

Rejoicing in the Spirit

LUKE 10:21-23

*In that same hour he rejoiced in the Holy Spirit
and said, "I thank you, Father, Lord of heaven
and earth, that you have hidden these things
from the wise and understanding and revealed
them to little children; yes, Father, for such was
your gracious will. All things have been handed
over to me by my Father, and no one knows who
the Son is except the Father, or who the Father
is except the Son and anyone to whom the Son
chooses to reveal him." Then turning to the
disciples he said privately, "Blessed are the
eyes that see what you see!"*

No one knows who the Son is except the Father, and
no one knows who the Father is except the Son and
those to whom the Son chooses to reveal him.

Lord God, I can hardly contain my joy and
thankfulness that you have chosen to reveal your Son
to me. I know that I have done nothing to gain your
attention. Indeed, I was bent on going my own way

42

and living for myself alone. There is nothing in me that you might have looked at and thought worthy of salvation. To all intents and purposes, I was your enemy.

Yet you reached down to me and spoke to my heart. You gave me understanding of your great mercy and love. Thank you for saving me. Thank you for not condemning me for my rejection of you. Thank you for changing my heart that I might love you and serve you.

This is what I want Lord. To love you more and to serve you in any way you wish me to serve. My heart is open to your will. Guide me in your paths Lord. Open my ears to your Word.

Even as Moses desired to see you Lord, I desire to see you and to know you more. Fill me with your Holy Spirit. Earnestly I seek you my Lord and my God, for you are above all things.

Thank you for this great salvation, in Jesus Name, Amen.

Nothing Except Christ Crucified

1 CORINTHIANS 2:1-16

And I, when I came to you, brothers, did not come proclaiming to you the testimony of God with lofty speech or wisdom. For I decided to know nothing among you except Jesus Christ and him crucified.

And I was with you in weakness and in fear and much trembling, and my speech and my message were not in plausible words of wisdom, but in demonstration of the Spirit and of power, so that your faith might not rest in the wisdom of men but in the power of God.

Yet among the mature we do impart wisdom, although it is not a wisdom of this age or of the rulers of this age, who are doomed to pass away. But we impart a secret and hidden wisdom of God, which God decreed before the ages for our glory. None of the rulers of this age understood this, for if they had, they would not have crucified the Lord of glory.

But, as it is written,

"What no eye has seen, nor ear heard, nor the heart of man imagined, what God has prepared for those who love him"— these things God has revealed to us through the Spirit.

For the Spirit searches everything, even the depths of God. For who knows a person's thoughts except the spirit of that person, which is in him? So also no one comprehends the thoughts of God except the Spirit of God.

Now we have received not the spirit of the world, but the Spirit who is from God, that we might understand the things freely given us by God.

And we impart this in words not taught by human wisdom but taught by the Spirit, interpreting spiritual truths to those who are spiritual.

The natural person does not accept the things of the Spirit of God, for they are folly to him, and he is not able to understand them because they are spiritually discerned.

The spiritual person judges all things, but is himself to be judged by no one. "For who has understood the mind of the Lord so as to instruct him?" But we have the mind of Christ.

Holy God, I bless you for giving me this new day. I pray that I will serve you well in whatever I say and whatever I do. I pray that my living will reflect my love of you.

Like the apostle Paul, I want to know nothing but Jesus Christ and Him crucified. I know that without the cross there is no life. Without the cross there is no hope and no future. Without the cross, all there is left is hell.

Yet with everything I have read of your gospel, I know that I understand so little. I know that the more I understand of your work on the cross, the more my life will be radically affected. I am ashamed of how little at times my life is affected by Jesus' sacrifice. Forgive me Father for not laying hold of your truth more earnestly. Give me a heart for your truth and show me your wisdom.

I pray that you will fill me with your Spirit so that my mind might be enlightened. I want to take hold of and affirm the gospel. Open and unveil my mind, correct and adjust my heart that I might understand what you have revealed.

I pray for my church. I pray that you will give us a greater understanding of the gospel. I know the more we understand, the more our hearts will be filled with desire to share about what you have done. Give us all a greater love for your word and more willingness to spend time searching and thinking about scripture.

I know that you have revealed yourself to mankind through your Word. I know that you have provided us with everything we need in the Bible as to how we need to live and how we need to serve you. Yet how often we fail to go to it. How often I fail to go to it.

I hate how I neglect the Bible at times. I know it is where you feed me and encourage me, yet I still don't spend enough time reading it. I pray your forgiveness and ask for a mind more fixed on you in Jesus Name, Amen.

I Will Extol You

PSALM 145

I will extol you, my God and King, and bless your name forever and ever. Every day I will bless you and praise your name forever and ever. Great is the LORD, and greatly to be praised, and his greatness is unsearchable.

One generation shall commend your works to another and shall declare your mighty acts. On the glorious splendor of your majesty, and on your wondrous works, I will meditate.

They shall speak of the might of your awesome deeds, and I will declare your greatness. They shall pour forth the fame of your abundant goodness and shall sing aloud of your righteousness.

The LORD is gracious and merciful, slow to anger and abounding in steadfast love. The LORD is good to all, and his mercy is over all that he has made.

All your works shall give thanks to you, O LORD, and all your saints shall bless you! They shall speak of the glory of your kingdom and tell of your power, to make known to the children of man your mighty deeds, and the glorious splendor of your kingdom. Your kingdom is an everlasting kingdom, and your dominion endures throughout all generations.

The LORD is faithful in all his words and kind in all his works. The LORD upholds all who are falling and raises up all who are bowed down. The eyes of all look to you, and you give them their food in due season.

You open your hand; you satisfy the desire of every living thing. The LORD is righteous in all his ways and kind in all his works. The LORD is near to all who call on him, to all who call on him in truth.

He fulfills the desire of those who fear him; he also hears their cry and saves them. The LORD preserves all who love him, but all the wicked he will destroy.

My mouth will speak the praise of the Lord, and let all flesh bless his holy name forever and ever.

From reading the Psalm, it is now my prayer.

Today I want to praise you Lord and thank you for all you have done. I will exalt you, my God, O king; and I will bless your name for ever and ever. Every day will I bless you; and will praise your name for ever and ever.

You are Lord, and greatly to be praised; your greatness is unsearchable. One generation shall praise your works to another and shall declare your mighty acts. I will speak of the glorious honor of your majesty, and of your wondrous works.

And men shall speak of the might of your awesome acts and declare your greatness. They shall abundantly utter the memory of your great goodness and shall sing of your righteousness.

You are gracious, and full of compassion; slow to anger, and of great mercy. You are good to all: and your tender mercies are over all your works. All your works bring you praise, O LORD; and I will bless you.

I will speak of the glory of your kingdom and proclaim your power. I will make known to those around me your mighty acts, and the glorious majesty of your kingdom.

Your kingdom is an everlasting kingdom, and your dominion endures throughout all generations. You uphold all that fall and raise up all those that be bowed down.

The eyes of all look to you; and you give them their meat in due season. You open your hand and satisfy the desire of every living thing.

You are LORD and are righteous in all your ways, and holy in all your works. You are near to all that call upon you, to all that call upon you in truth. You will fulfill the desire of those that fear you: you will hear their cry and save them. You look after all those that love you.

My mouth shall speak the praise of the LORD: I will bless your holy name for ever and ever. Amen.

Living Sacrifices

ROMANS 12:1-8

I appeal to you therefore, brothers, by the mercies of God, to present your bodies as a living sacrifice, holy and acceptable to God, which is your spiritual worship.

Do not be conformed to this world, but be transformed by the renewal of your mind, that by testing you may discern what is the will of God, what is good and acceptable and perfect.

For by the grace given to me I say to everyone among you not to think of himself more highly than he ought to think, but to think with sober judgment, each according to the measure of faith that God has assigned.

For as in one body we have many members, and the members do not all have the same function, so we, though many, are one body in Christ, and individually members one of another.

Having gifts that differ according to the grace given to us, let us use them: if prophecy, in proportion to our faith; if service, in our

serving; the one who teaches, in his teaching;
the one who exhorts, in his exhortation; the one
who contributes, in generosity; the one who
leads, with zeal; the one who does acts of mercy,
with cheerfulness.

You O Lord are high above all the earth; you are exalted above all things. There is nothing that can compare to you. Nothing that comes anywhere close to your incredible love and mercy. You deserve everything that I can give.

I offer my life to you Lord as a living sacrifice. My whole life. My sleeping, my eating, my work, my family, I offer it all up to you. My thoughts, my feelings, my desires, my speech, I offer it all up to you. I have nothing else.

Please take my life and let it be a love song in your honor. I cannot express the gratitude I have in my heart for all you have done for me. I am your slave, do with me as you will.

I desire to be obedient to you. Give me a heart that I might follow you. Give me love for others, as you have loved me. Teach me how I might show others what it is you have done for them. Use me to bring honor to your Name.

I really want to be useful to you for the sake of your kingdom. Help me work with others to further your work. Make me sensitive to your will that I might obey. I pray for spiritual gifts that I might be a blessing to your body. Especially I pray for wisdom. I want to help those around me and be a friend to those in need. I want to reveal you to others through my actions.

I pray for opportunity to share about you. I pray for opportunity to pray with others. I pray for opportunity to encourage and love.

I pray that you will forgive me for the times that I have been too busy, or embarrassed or uncaring to take hold of opportunities you have given me in the past. I don't want this in my life. Please help me to see and take hold of those moments when you bring people across my path. I pray again for wisdom.

Father fill me with your Holy Spirit. I pray that you will refresh me and encourage my heart, in Jesus Name, Amen.

Crowned with Glory
and Honour

PSALM 8:3-5

*When I look at your heavens, the work of your
fingers, the moon and the stars, which you have
set in place, what is man that you are mindful of
him, and the son of man that you care for him?*

*Yet you have made him a little lower than the
heavenly beings and crowned him with glory
and honor.*

Holy God, I thank you for this new day. I commit it
into your hands and pray that you will guide me.
Direct me in my speech and in my actions. I love you
Lord and I want to bring honor to you today. You
are my creator, the one who knows the deep things
of my heart.

You knit me together in my mother's womb and had
my days ordained before I was even born. You chose
to reveal yourself to me and in doing so made me a

part of your great plans and purposes to bring glory to your name.

What is man, that you are mindful of him? and the son of man, that you visit him?

For you have made him a little lower than the angels and have crowned him with glory and honor.

It is incredible to me that you have chosen a people who hated you, who turned their backs on you and betrayed you to be the ones whom you use to display your greatness and faithfulness. What indeed is man that you are mindful of him?

I know that there is nothing about us that turned you towards us. There is nothing that was deserving of being saved, yet you, in your great mercy and kindness, chose to take the veil from our eyes and give us sight.

You chose to reveal yourself to us and remove our sins from us as far as the east is from the west. Then you gave us a new heart and a new desire in life.

I thank you so much that you have done this in my life. I thank you for my church and the brothers and sisters you have given me in your family.

I am your servant Lord and I pray that you will give me wisdom to do the works you want me to do. I pray that I will bring encouragement and comfort to those around me. I pray that my life will always point others towards you that they too might experience your great love. In Jesus Name, Amen.

Father of Glory

*For this reason, because I have heard of your
faith in the Lord Jesus and your love toward all
the saints,*

*I do not cease to give thanks for you,
remembering you in my prayers, that the God of
our Lord Jesus Christ, the Father of glory, may
give you the Spirit of wisdom and of revelation
in the knowledge of him, having the eyes of your
hearts enlightened, that you may know what is
the hope to which he has called you,*

*what are the riches of his glorious inheritance
in the saints, and what is the immeasurable
greatness of his power toward us who believe,*

*according to the working of his great might that
he worked in Christ when he raised him from
the dead and seated him at his right hand in the
heavenly places,*

*far above all rule and authority and power and
dominion, and above every name that is named,
not only in this age but also in the one to come.*

And he put all things under his feet and gave
him as head over all things to the church, which
is his body, the fullness of him who fills
all in all.

Holy God, I pray that you will give me the Spirit of wisdom and revelation, so that I might know you more. My heart's desire is that I might see your face, understand your ways, and walk in your paths. I pray that I might gain deep insight into your work and the rich gifts you give me in Christ.

I pray that the eyes of my heart might be enlightened so that I might know the hope to which you have called me. That as I read your word, I might understand the gospel deep within my spirit. Help me to grow daily in understanding what you have done for me so that I might appreciate you more. Thank you that my future is secure, that I need not fear death but know that I will spend eternity with you.

I thank you that you live within me and guide me into your truth. I pray that I will see more of your power at work in my life for your glory.

It is incredible to me that the same power that raised Christ from the dead is at work in my life. It is incredible to me that you give me an inheritance and that I am precious in your sight. Who is there like you Lord, and who can understand you?

Thank you, O God, for your great kindness and mercy.

Thank you for the strength you give me. That I need never walk alone as you will never forsake me. You strengthen me to go through each day, no matter how difficult something is, you are always there. Words are just not enough to say how much I love you.

Give me more wisdom Lord. Give me more revelation of you in Jesus Name, Amen.

Strengthened with Power

EPHESIANS 3:14-21

*For this reason, I bow my knees before the
Father, from whom every family in heaven and
on earth is named,*

*that according to the riches of his glory he may
grant you to be strengthened with power
through his Spirit in your inner being, so that
Christ may dwell in your hearts through faith,*

*that you, being rooted and grounded in love,
may have strength to comprehend with all the
saints what is the breadth and length and height
and depth, and to know the love of Christ that
surpasses knowledge, that you may be filled
with all the fullness of God.*

*Now to him who is able to do far more
abundantly than all that we ask or think,
according to the power at work within us,*

*to him be glory in the church and in Christ
Jesus throughout all generations, forever and
ever. Amen.*

O God glorify your name in all the earth. Let all creation praise your name. Let the sun, moon and stars declare your majesty. Your holiness and goodness is beyond compare. Your acts are incomprehensible to me. Who is there like you? Who is there that can understand you? You are my Lord and my God. You are the desire of my heart.

Father I pray that you might strengthen me with power by your Spirit in my innermost being. Without you at work in my life, I have no reason to live. No reason to face each day. You are everything to me.

I pray that you will give me more understanding of the mystery that you dwell within me. I am so blessed by this, but I know that I understand nothing. I know that the more I comprehend this, the more my life will change to glorify you. I pray that you will deepen my faith.

How often I have thought it would have been wonderful to have walked with Jesus on this earth and seen him face to face. How blind I have been to not see that your dwelling in me is the same thing. Never a moment passes that you are not with me, that you help, comfort and bring great joy and peace.

You have rooted and established me in love and now I pray that you will give me grace to grasp how wide and long and high and deep is the love of Christ for me. I want to know this love that surpasses knowledge, I want to be filled with all the fullness of God.

You are able to do immeasurably more than anything I could ask or imagine. Work in my life Lord. Change my heart and help me to grow to be more like you, in Jesus Name, Amen.

Praise the Lord!

*Praise the Lord! I will give thanks to the Lord
with my whole heart, in the company of the
upright, in the congregation. Great are the
works of the Lord, studied by all who delight in
them.*

*Full of splendor and majesty is his work, and his
righteousness endures forever. He has caused
his wondrous works to be remembered; the Lord
is gracious and merciful.*

*He provides food for those who fear him; he
remembers his covenant forever. He has shown
his people the power of his works, in giving
them the inheritance of the nations.*

*The works of his hands are faithful and just; all
his precepts are trustworthy; they are
established forever and ever, to be performed
with faithfulness and uprightness. He sent
redemption to his people; he has commanded
his covenant forever. Holy and awesome is his
name! The fear of the Lord is the beginning of*

O Lord, I praise you with all of my heart. Give me grace to declare your glory before all my family and friends.

Your deeds are great and are thought about by all that love you. Your works are glorious and majestic, and your righteousness endures for ever.

You have caused your wonders to be remembered. You O God are gracious and compassionate. You provide for all who fear you and your faithfulness lasts for ever.

You have shown the power of your works among those who believe and those who don't. The works of your hands are faithful and just and all your laws are trustworthy.

Your works are steadfast and are done in faithfulness and uprightness. Your salvation has come into my life and for that I will bless your name for ever.

As I read your word, I realize more and more how little I understand of you. How little I know you. Father I pray again, reveal yourself to me. Draw me close to you.

Give me grace to share of your works to those around me. Gift me with words that will bring glory to your name. Move in your power in my life that your name will be lifted up and people turn to you.

I pray that my life might be a witness to you. Let the way I live my life and my love for you touch those around me so that they will be drawn to you.

I want to be obedient. Open my understanding and soften my heart, in Jesus Name, Amen.

Reconciled by the Son

ROMANS 5:9-10

Since, therefore, we have now been justified by his blood, much more shall we be saved by him from the wrath of God.

For if while we were enemies we were reconciled to God by the death of his Son, much more, now that we are reconciled, shall we be saved by his life.

O God, if your mercy had limits, to whom could I go to escape your wrath? Yet your love toward me in Christ is without measure. I thank you that I can come before you and ask forgiveness for my sins.

Forgive me for the times I have gone my own way and done my own thing and ignored your voice trying to turn me back to what was right. Forgive me for the times that by doing nothing, I have done wrong. Forgive me for the works I did not do, for the kindness I did not give and the comfort I did not extend.

I thank you for the work of your Son Jesus who took the full measure of your wrath against me so that I might not be condemned. How great is your mercy and grace.

I pray that I might love you more fervently every day. I want my service toward you to be more sincere and my life wholly devoted to you. That is my desire.

I know that I stumble and backslide in my commitment toward you. I know that I am weak, but you lift me up, you restore me and you continue to love me and give me hope.

I pray each day that I live you will help me to change, help me to hate and flee from evil. Help me to overcome those sins that I so easily slip into. Help me to be more determined, more watchful, and more prayerful.

I ask that no evil will come from the times when I have sinned against you. Let no-one's heart be hardened because of my foolishness and pride. I want my life to honor you, in Jesus Name, Amen.

My Soul Thirsts for You

PSALM 143:5-6

I remember the days of old; I meditate on all that you have done; I ponder the work of your hands. I stretch out my hands to you; my soul thirsts for you like a parched land.

Holy Father, you know that I long for nothing but you. I desire with all my heart to live a holy life and to live according to your will.

I know that these desires come from you and that only you can fulfill them. I want my whole life to be under subjection to you and I want nothing corrupt or ungodly in my life.

I am so blessed that you are changing my heart and that you are making me more aware of your will.

You are giving me ears that hear and a heart that listens. Help me not to be satisfied with little and become complacent in my walk with you.

Help me to draw closer to you, to love, to long and plead with you. Help me to wrestle with things I don't understand rather than give up. Help me to strive for holiness of life and heart.

O God wrap my life in divine love and keep my heart fresh in desiring you. I pray for a humbleness of character and a willingness to follow you no matter what the cost.

I know that every good thing that I am inclined to do, and every good thought comes from you. I know that it is your grace that enables me to grow in my love for you.

You are indescribable Lord. Words alone cannot express how wonderful you are. I love you Lord and I pray that each day will bring new understanding of you, in Jesus Name, Amen.

Who is Like You?

EXODUS 15:11

Who is like you, O Lord, among the gods? Who is like you, majestic in holiness, awesome in glorious deeds, doing wonders?

Holy God, I pray that whether in public or private, whether at work or home, that my life might be steeped in prayer and filled with the Spirit. That with each prayer I will be more aware of Jesus' atoning blood and the price that was paid for me.

I pray that your help and presence will be with me all the days of my life until that time when I will see you face to face and behold your glory.

You fuel my need for you, your promises invite me into your presence and called by your Spirit I am drawn to worship you. O God, you are great in majesty, glorious in holiness and full of wonder. Your love surrounds me and my heart is lifted by you.

There is nothing in me that deserves this great salvation. I know that I was guilty and that I had nothing with which to repay you, yet you decided in your great love and mercy to make a way for mankind to come to you. I thank you that through the precious blood of your Son I am redeemed. I was bought at a terrible price.

I pray that you will bless me by revealing to me more of the things you have done. Speak peace into my repentant heart. Give me desire that I might give you no rest until every thought, every word and deed comes under your authority. I pray for a purified heart and a growing faith to overcome the pull of the world.

I pray that I might be filled with love for others and that my love for you and my awareness of the cross grows daily, in Jesus Name, Amen.

Surrounded by Witnesses

*Therefore, since we are surrounded by so great
a cloud of witnesses, let us also lay aside every
weight, and sin which clings so closely,*

*and let us run with endurance the race that is
set before us, looking to Jesus, the founder and
perfecter of our faith, who for the joy that was
set before him endured the cross, despising the
shame, and is seated at the right hand of the
throne of God.*

*Consider him who endured from sinners such
hostility against himself, so that you may not
grow weary or fainthearted.*

O God, you alone are the maker of heaven and earth.
You are creator God who spoke the world into being
and still sustain every living thing by the word of
your mouth.

How great are your works and the sum of them. Your
faithfulness and goodness is spoken from generation

to generation and your works declare your mercy and grace. I love you Lord.

I pray that I might live for you. That I might never be satisfied with what I have and that I might constantly seek to be more like you. I want to constantly seek to conform to your word and have my actions reflect what I believe. I pray that as I learn more of you, that my life will be one of obedience and delight in you.

I ask that you keep me running the race of faith. That I might never give up until I hear your words at the final step 'well done good and faithful servant'.

Support me so when my strength fails you will raise me up and once again encourage my heart. I never want to turn back or enjoy fleeting pleasures that disappear into nothing. You are everything to me.

I pray that as I walk with you, by your grace let me be someone whose sole aim is a burning desire for you and you alone. I ask this in Jesus Name, Amen.

Transformed

ROMANS 12:2

*Do not be conformed to this world, but be
transformed by the renewal of your mind, that
by testing you may discern what is the will of
God, what is good and acceptable and perfect.*

Heavenly Father look after me and guide me this day.
Without your leading I stray into all sorts of wrong
doing. I pray that you will hedge my path so that I
might not wander into disobedience.

I pray that you will incline my heart to your ways.
Shape me into the image of your Son. I am as clay
in your hands.

Make me aware of anything in my life that I need to
let go of - anything that does not honor you.

I pray especially for my speech. I pray that I might
speak to my family and those around me with
kindness, and that your goodness will shine through
my life. I pray that I will be a blessing and a witness

to those around me. I pray that my love for your word will grow stronger. That I will not be able to live or breathe without it. I know that your words bring life and light and that your words sustain me. Forgive me for the many times I have neglected to listen to you and instead filled my hours with meaningless activities.

Forgive me for the many times I have put other works ahead of you and indeed even made idols of them. I know there have been many times when I have been lukewarm toward you. There have been many moments of unbelief. I pray that you will forgive me and root those moments out of my life. I want to live a life of faith and not believe one minute and disbelieve the next. I want my life to be on fire for you.

I pray that you will transform me by the renewing of my mind. I pray that as I read your word it will pierce deep into my spirit and change me to be more like you.

I ask you that I will see everything in the light of eternity and long for the coming of my Savior so I might truly live as if each day were my last. I know that without you I can do nothing. You are my Lord and my God. I ask you these things in Jesus Name, Amen.

Planted by Streams

PSALM 1

Blessed is the man who walks not in the counsel
of the wicked, nor stands in the way of sinners,
nor sits in the seat of scoffers; but his delight is
in the law of the Lord, and on his law he
meditates day and night.

He is like a tree planted by streams of water that
yields its fruit in its season, and its leaf does not
wither. In all that he does, he prospers. The
wicked are not so, but are like chaff that the
wind drives away.

Therefore the wicked will not stand in the
judgment, nor sinners in the congregation of the
righteous; for the Lord knows the way of the
righteous, but the way of the wicked will perish.

Father I thank you for your grace, thank you for your
word. Thank you that your word is not dead but that
it is alive and powerful. Thank you that because of
the work of Christ on the cross, the veil has been
lifted and I can see you face to face. I can see the

wonderful works that you have done through men and women throughout the ages. I pray that you will glorify yourself by such works through me and my family.

I pray that you will continue to open my eyes. I pray that you will give me a mind that is filled with light and filled with the knowledge of your word. I ask that I might know you. I don't want to be a passive church goer, but I want to be someone who reflects your character in all the different circumstances in my life. I want to be of service in the body.

I pray for spiritual gifts for the benefit of the church.

I pray that I might grow in faith and grow in love and in the knowledge of you. I ask that I won't be as a 'stunted tree' but rather be like a giant oak. Someone who is deeply rooted and grounded in your love.

I pray that I might be like the man in this Psalm. That I will not walk in the counsel of the wicked or stand in the way of sinners or sit in the seat of mockers. Instead, I want my delight to be in your law. I want your word to be in my mind and heart day and night.

O God, I want to be filled with your Spirit and be like that tree that yields its fruit in season. I want the fruit of the Spirit to be evident in my life. I want others to be blessed by my walk with you. I ask this in Jesus Name, Amen.

For God so Loved...

JOHN 3:16

For God so loved the world, that he gave his only Son, that whoever believes in him should not perish but have eternal life.

O God of grace help me to pray in faith and so find your will. Help me to lean on your mercy and believe in your promises.

Strengthen me to pray with unwavering belief, that whatever I receive is a gift from you, and that I might pray steadfastly until you answer. I pray that I might be like the woman who wouldn't give up until the judge had answered her.

Help me to be completely dependent on you. Guide me by your Spirit and make me sensitive to His leading. I want to walk in your paths and learn your ways so that my life might reflect your love. All for your honor and all for your glory.

I pray that my love for you will grow. I know that I can't make myself love you more. I know that every iota of love and service that I give to you is only because you have first worked in my heart. Always, your work comes first.

Father I pray that you will constantly bring my thoughts to the cross. I pray that I will know nothing except Christ and him crucified.

I pray that you will give me wisdom to understand and words to share your immeasurable love with others. Give me a heart of compassion for the lost. Give me a desire to intercede and pray for those that are without hope.

I pray that you will open hearts and that you will show again and again your great mercy to those around me. Save my family Lord, save my friends, save my colleagues at work. Let your grace abound in their lives. Let your mercy be shown toward them.

I pray for the Church. That we might constantly seek your face. That we might never be complacent but strive after you with all our heart, mind, soul and strength. I pray that we might ever be found about our Father's business, in Jesus Name I pray, Amen.

What's Next?

You have reached the end of *Daily Prayer Seeking the Heart of God!*

So now what?

How about praying through *Daily Prayer Pursuing Holiness*?

Or one of these next three that take you on a prayer journey through a whole book of the Bible?

- *Daily Prayer through the Life of Jesus (Luke)*
- *Daily Prayer Taking up the Shield of Faith (Ephesians)*
- *Daily Prayer Drawing near the Throne of Grace (Hebrews)*

Just do a search for *Berenice Aguilera*, and you will find them easily.

***

If you like to write down Bible verses and prayers, you might enjoy using this set of journals.

Taking the time to write out scripture, slowing everything down by thinking, and maybe studying the verses, before praying through them will make a big difference, both to growing in the knowledge of God, and drawing close to Him.

BLACK JOURNAL FOR WOMEN

BLACK JOURNAL FOR MEN

ORANGE FLOWER SERIES

PARCHMENT SERIES

In each journal there is a page to write out a short Bible passage, followed by a page for reflection on what you have read and written, and a page for your prayers.

Once you have gone through the whole journal, you will have written, thought, and prayed through the whole of at least one book of the Bible.

Each journal comes in a choice of four covers. Two with plain interiors, and two with a more detailed design.

They are available for the following books of the Bible:

Galatians

Ephesians

Philippians

Colossians

1 & 2 Thessalonians

1 & 2 Timothy, Titus, Philemon

James

1 & 2 Peter

1, 2, 3 John & Jude

These journals are easily found by searching for *Berenice Aguilera Journals.*

Made in United States
Troutdale, OR
02/20/2024

17831641R00055